Bro. Dominic Berardelli, F.S.C.
Special Assistant to the President
Saint Mary's College
P.O. Box 4300
Moraga, CA 94575-4300

215.-

D0731084

A GOLDEN
SOUVENIR
OF THE

HILLTRIBES

OF THAILAND

Photography and Text by Michael Freeman

Published by Asia Books Co.
5 Soi 61 Sukhumvit Rd.
Bangkok, Thailand
Tel. 391-2680
Fax (662) 381-1621

Right
A young Lahu Sheh Leh boy wearing a miniature version of the distinctive black cotton tunic bordered with white. Close-fitting embroidered caps for children are a Lahu speciality.

Page 6-7
A late October storm breaks over the mountains near Mae Hong Son, in the far northwest of Thailand. The hill-country which is home to the six tribal groups is in the sub-tropical monsoon belt. The rains normally begin in May and continue until the end of October, dropping around 50 inches (1250mm) of precipitation during this period.

Page 8-9
The Akha village of Mae Cha'Akha, half a mile from the Burmese border in Chiang Rai Province. In the middle of the dry season, tribes begin to clear new fields by burning sections of forests. In the still, dry air, the pall of smoke lingers day after day, and the sun shines a pale yellow through the haze.

Page 10-11
Embroidery details of a cotton shoulder bag, with modern plastic buttons and forest seeds sewn on for extra decoration. Needlework of various styles is one of the now infamous traditional crafts among the women of all the hilltribes.

Text and photography by Michael Freemann

Color Separations by Bangkok 71 Film
Typeset by CompuPrint
Designed by Christopher C. Burt

Printed in China

ISBN# 974-8206-41-6

INTRODUCTION

THE HILLTRIBES OF THAILAND

The heartland of Southeast Asia has always been on the edges of civilization. The great empires, such as Pagan in Burma, Sukhothai in Thailand and Angkor in Cambodia, were built in the plains, where rice grows easily and there are trade routes to the sea. For the rulers of the time - as well as for the governments of today - the writ of law petered out in the jumble of limestone hills and teak forests of the north. From the Tibetan Plateau, of the Himalayas, several great ranges of mountains flow out in a big curve, first east, then sweeping southward. Lying between them are the upper reaches of three great Asian rivers - the Yangtze, Mekong and Salween. Where these rivers diverge, the hill-country spills out in a disorganized mass, around the borders of Burma, China, Laos and Thailand.

The roads, even today, are pathetically inadequate, and trails winding from ridge to ridge are the normal means of contact and transport. Dusty in the dry season, slippery with mud in the wet, they link hamlet to hamlet across hundreds of miles of broken terrain. Little wonder that these hills have long had a reputation for lawlessness and intrigue, from the fiercely independent princes of Burma's Shan States to roving mercenary armies. Their remoteness has also made them the stronghold of mainland Asia's last ethnic minorities - the hilltribes.

Until recently, Thailand was the only country in which it was possible for travellers to visit hilltribe villages, and is still the only country without travel restrictions. As a result, the six principal tribes who have settled in Thailand are by far the best known, but there are, in the Yunnan of China and Burma in particular, many others. Their ethnic diversity and highly distinctive cultures makes them some of the most intriguing and appealing minorities anywhere in the world, all the more so in the face of what is happening to the towns and cities of Southeast Asia. The street life of Bangkok has changed almost out of recognition in the last two decades, with expensive cars, department stores and condominiums as prominent as in any other major world city, but life in the more remote hilltribe villages has altered little in centuries. For tourists who are looking for more than just a beach holiday in Thailand, trekking in the North has become one of the country's major attractions.

The main area of hill-country in Thailand is the exotically-named Golden Triangle - along the borders with Burma and northwest Laos and the confluence of the Mekong and Mae Kok rivers - and this is where most of the tribal groups are concentrated. In the settlement of the North, they are newcomers; the main migration started only at the beginning of this century. A consensus of studies put the hilltribe population at a little short of half a million in 1983, most of this since the end of the Second World War. The Karen (known to the Thais as Karieng and Yang) arrived from the west, across the lower Salween River in Burma. The Lisu (Lisaw in Thai), Lahu (Muser) and Akha (Eekaw) crossed into Thailand mainly from Burma's Shan State in the north, while the Hmong (Meo) and Mien (Yao) crossed over the Mekong River from Laos. These migrations are, however, just the final stages of a much longer history of movement, and the ultimate origins of most of the tribes is shrouded in uncertainty. And, as none except the Mien have written records, there is little chance of unveiling their early history.

The oral tradition, though, is strong, and at times the epic poems and complex genealogies give tantalising glimpses of social upheavals and great journeys in the distant past. Certain Hmong legends, for example, recount cold lands with long winter nights, which might suggest northern Asia or the Tibetan plateau, while the Mien have a legend concerning a sea crossing, which might have been from southeast China.

A forest giant, left standing over the central village square when the land was originally cleared for settlement, is silhouetted against a winter's dawn sky. Village life has already begun before first light, and women and girls are on their way to fetch water from the spring.

In a world without electricity and machine tools virtually everthing the hilltribe people create is still done by hand. At top, a Lisu man prepares a forest net trap. A Lahu Na women stitches embroidery (middle), and an Akha girl threads Job's Tear seeds into a necklace (bottom).

Long recitations, committed to memory and passed on from generation to generation are, in fact, essential for continuing the culture. Among the Akha, for example, it is important for a man to be able to remember his complete genealogy, right back to the first man, Sm Mi O, and this now covers more than 60 generations. Although the beginning of these genealogies is as much absorbed in legend and religion as is the Book of Genesis in the Christian Old Testament, the surprising thing is how closely they correspond with one another. Genealogies and other histories from Akha in different countries have similarities so close as to confirm their accuracy. All this, remarkably, is passed on by word of mouth, but such feats of memory are an everyday skill among peoples who have had no other means of preserving their past.

One thing is certain about the history of all the hilltribes. They have been forced to migrate in order to survive. The hills of the Golden Triangle are beautiful enough on trekking holidays, but are nobody's first choice for a home. The land is poor for farming, and the terrain difficult. These ethnic minorities are tribes of the hills because, for centuries past they have retreated in the face of stronger lowland peoples. Leading an unsettled life in the forested hills, always at risk of having to move further on, has been the only way of keeping their cultural identity - and this is something that all the hilltribes feel very strongly. Just a day or two spent with a hilltribe community is enough for even a casual visitor to see how highly they value the uniqueness of their own way of life.

KAREN

The six main tribes are each distinct, not only in the obvious way of their costume, but also in their rituals and approach to life. The Karen, for instance, differ from all the other groups now in Thailand in showing no traces of contact with the Chinese. Although it is possible that they came originally from Southwest China or Tibet, there is no hard evidence, and their homeland is, to all intents, now Burma. As well as settling in the north of Thailand - in the provinces of Chiang Mai, Chiang Rai and Mae Hong Son - the Karen have also moved south as far as the isthmus south and west of Bangkok.

In Burma itself, it is the mainly Christian Karen who have led the struggle for ethnic independence from the Burmese in a low-grade civil war that has lasted almost since the departure of the British. The continuing fighting regularly spills over into Thailand, and encourages more migration - illegal to the Thai government's point of view. Half a million Karen have crossed into Thailand, making them by far the most populous of the hilltribe groups. This sometimes surprises visitors to the North, as the Karen are a little less colourful in appearance than other tribes, and are often less open to outsiders, even though hospitable. Visually less prominent in their appearance, the Karen also seem less forceful and distinctive in other aspects of their culture. They readily adopt lowland Thai farming, men's dress and house-building techniques, the language has absorbed many words from Thai and Burmese, among others, while a number of Karen legends follow themes of being down-trodden and oppressed.

Nevertheless, although Karen girls' dress cannot compete in flamboyance with that of a Lisu or Akha, they are renowned and expert weavers. The clothes of the two Karen cultures found in Thailand - Sgaw and Pwo - differ slightly, with the Pwo being more elaborate. The upper garment, whether short or long, or for men, women or children, has the same simple construction: two strips of cloth, one folded over the left shoulder, the other over the right, stitched together at the front and back. Before marriage, girls wear white, but the blouse and sarong of married women vary considerably in pattern and colour. Overall, however, red predominates.

For married women of both sub-groups, the dress is the relatively simple (for hilltribes) combination of a blouse and a long, sarong-style skirt. Often it is the lower part of the blouse that is embroidered, while some Pwo designs are particularly strong, with bright, large motifs. The skirts are sewn into tubes from two pieces of material - tie-dyeing, in which the threads are first bound at intervals and dipped in dye before being used, is a common technique, particularly among those Karen living at higher altitudes.

As with all the tribes, it is the women who conserve the traditions of dress, and most Karen men have abandoned the traditional smock, sarong and calf-length pants in favour of modern Thai and western dress. Tattooing is the main ornament for men, although less so among the young.

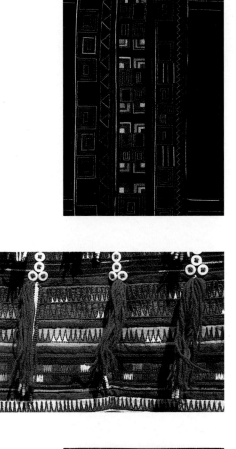

Beads of all kinds make up an important part of Karen jewellery, and some women can be seen wearing a mass of bead necklaces that covers the breast and half of the shoulders. Another particularly Karen style of ornament among those women who can afford it is a stack of silver bracelets of different designs, all the way up the arms if possible. This effect recalls the highly peculiar decoration of one Karen sub-group found mainly in Burma - neck rings. Padaung women traditionally wear permanently-worn rings that are added regularly from girlhood. The stack of thick rings slowly pushes down on the collar-bone to give the appearance of a strangely elongated neck. Because of fighting between the Karen and the Burmese Army, a few Padaung families have settled in the Mae Hong Son area.

Among both Sgaw and Pwo, there are two kinds of village location: mountain and valley. In Thailand, most Karen live in mountain villages because of land scarcity, and they practice, in common with the other hilltribes, shifting agriculture (also called swiddening and slash-and-burn). This method, which involves clearing new forest regularly, depends on being able to return the fields to fallow after a year of crops - for anything up to a decade, Now, however, population pressure on the land makes this kind of husbandry almost impossible.

Karen houses are stilted, usually with one room and a large, well-used verandah. There are no household altars; instead, some way outside the village there is a shrine to the local deity, the Lord of Land and Water.

Lisu

The Lisu's flamboyantly colourful dress reflects an innate competitiveness that surfaces in other ways as well. Above leggings and Chinese-style pants, the women wear a broad-sleeved, multi-coloured tunic. This, with a predominant colour of either blue or green, crosses the chest and is fastened under the right arm, hanging knee-length at the front and rather lower at the back. Red sleeves, bands of other material, and large quantities of silver, at times of celebration, complete the outfit. The men's costume is a black jacket and blue or green pants. Headdress, now worn mainly at festivals, is a broad, tasselled, silk turban. Preoccupied with looking their best, the Lisu are the sartorial peacocks of the hills.

The first Lisu families seem to have arrived in Thailand at the beginning of the century, though the first real wave of migration was probably in the 1920s. Although originally from southwest China, where much greater numbers still live, the Lisu in Thailand have all crossed over from Burma, and number around 20,000. Noticeably less withdrawn than other tribal groups in their dealings with outsiders, the Lisu are outspoken, and competitive to the point of conflict between clans. Like some of the Hmong, Mien and Lahu, certain Lisu villages grow opium as a cash crop, and so are the focus of Thai government efforts to reform.

Opium is one important factor in siting a Lisu village, many of which tend to be quite high in the mountains, at about 1000 metres or

Intricate embroidery is one of the hallmarks of hilltribe textiles. Although natural dyes are still used by some tribes, synthetic colors have come to replace them; not only do the new dyes save the trouble of having to collect and then process the traditional natural pigments but the hilltribe people genuinely prefer the brighter hues of the synthetics.

more. The opium poppy thrives best in this region at altitudes of around 1500 metres. Houses are built both on stilts and directly on the ground (with a floor of solid earth). Prominently located within the main living area, opposite the door, is the ancestral altar, and this is the focus of many household ceremonies. The spirits, some of whom are the ancestors worshipped at this altar, are part of a Lisu religious hierarchy, which includes a supreme being (Wu Sa), a god of healing and sickness, and a village guardian. This last has a shrine devoted to it in every village, with a roofed-over shelf for offerings and set in a small fenced area.

HMONG

The Hmong, of whom about 60,000 have settled in the country, are the second most populous of the hilltribes, although there are still much fewer than there are of the Karen. They are spread over a wide area of northern, and even central, Thailand, but most are concentrated in Chiang Mai, Chiang Rai, Petchabun and Tak provinces. They first started to settle in Thailand around the turn of the century, in common with most of the hill peoples, but are now found in such a large area of the country mainly because of a strong desire to acquire land. From the point of view of other tribes settled close to their villages, the Hmong seem, in fact, greedy for land, and in the modern conditions of land shortage, this leads, not infrequently, to conflict.

To some extent, all of the hilltribes have migrated because of political pressures, but for the Hmong this has dominated their history. In the recent past their main area of settlement has been southern China (where there are still about four million of them known by the name Miao) but before that it seems that they lived along the Yellow River, and possibly earlier still in the central Asian steppes. It is open to question whether life in the steppes, which have bred some notably tough and independently-minded peoples, has contributed to the Hmong character, but they have fought repeatedly against subjugation. Conflicts with the Chinese in the last century and in this (against the Kuomintang) caused migrations, originally into Laos. Many Hmong then fought with the Americans during the Vietnam War, and suffered further repression as a result.

Not surprisingly, then, the Hmong have the reputation of being the most independent of the hilltribes, and the ones whose lives seem the least influenced by visitors to their villages. They generally look down on other hilltribes, with the exception of the Mien, who are the other culture that has absorbed a considerable amount of Chinese influence. Many Hmong settlements rely heavily on opium as a cash crop, and so settle high in the hills. Continued pressure from government agencies and the Thai Royal Family's projects has, however, encouraged growing numbers to settle down and farm more conventional and acceptable crops.

The two main sub-groups in Thailand are the Blue Hmong and White Hmong, named, as is common, after differences in dress. (In fact, the Hmong's own term for the 'Blue' branch means 'Green Hmong'). Hmong needlework is particularly fine and richly detailed, and adorns all kinds of clothing, from the front of jackets and hem of skirts to children's caps and baby-carrying cloths.

The skirt of Blue Hmong women is pleated and quite short, reaching the knees. The central part is batiked with beeswax and dyed in indigo - hence the base colour is blue. The hem, like the front opening of the short jacket and the collar, is made from attached embroidered strips. The skirt of White Hmong women is, by contrast, of plain white hemp, also pleated, but nowadays tends to be worn only for ceremonial occasions. Hmong men of both branches wear loose, Chinese-style black pants and a short, partly embroidered black jacket fairly similar to that of the women.

(Top) A Lisu spirit offering used in a healing ceremony on a trail leading to the village

(Middle) Horn-like gable ends recall the galae decorations on northern Thai houses

(Bottom) Lashing cross-members of a roof during communal house-building

In appearance, however, the most eye-catching feature of Hmong women is their hair, which is tied up in a bun on top of the head. To this is sometimes added a strip of cloth or a turban. White Hmong women enhance the high-piled look of their hair by shaving the forehead. Some men still shave their heads to leave a queue falling from the crown.

The family and clan are the strongest social units, and the house itself has a strong family significance. Unlike most other hilltribe dwellings, Hmong houses are not stilted, but built directly on the earth, which is beaten down to make the floor of the large living area. The fire in the main hearth is supposed to be perpetual (when the family moves, live embers are carried to the next site) and the afterbirths of the family's children are buried in the floor by the father. The main living room is large enough to contain most daily activities, including the treadle rice pounder, which in a stilted house would normally be underneath.

Hmong worship is mainly directed towards a variety of household spirits, of which the spirit of the door is particularly important. In addition, the Hmong believe in a local deity who rules the surrounding area of forest and hill.

MIEN

The Mien, or Yao as called by the Thais and other hilltribes, are if anything even more strongly influenced by Chinese culture than the Hmong. Properly referred to by themselves as Iu Mien, their origins lie in southern China, at least as far as it is possible to tell. More than a million still live there, but migrant settlements are found in Vietnam, Laos and Thailand. There are about half as many Mien as Hmong in the country - around 30,000 - and most are settled north of Chiang Rai and in Phayao province. They first moved into Thailand in the middle-to-late nineteenth century, from Laos.

Apart from their dress, which to the first-time visitor is always the most identifiable feature of a hilltribe, the Mien stand apart from all the other tribal peoples in that they have adopted, and preserved, Chinese script. The Karen, Lisu, Akha and others show no sign of a written culture, even though it is possible that some may have had one in the past. The written tradition among the Mien has had an important effect - written records and sacred texts have to a large extent replaced the need to commit history and religion to memory.

There are no sub-groups within the Mien, so that there is little major difference in dress and appearance. The two most distinctive parts of the women's outfit are the black turban and the red ruff which, although it is actually sewn into the front edge and collar of the tunic, looks rather like an old-fashioned boa. The black or dark-blue tunic reaches the ankles, and underneath are worn heavily embroidered pants. A broad sash completes the dress.

Men's clothing is much less elaborate: Chinese-style loose-fitting pants and a fairly loose jacket, both either black or dark blue in village-woven cotton cloth. Young children wear fully-embroidered skull caps that are adorned with red woollen pom-poms (made in the same way as the women's ruffs).

Like the Hmong, Mien houses are built directly on the ground, and the main room has the same large proportions. There are other similarities: the rice pounder is located inside the main room, wood is used for the walls if available, and the house itself has strong spiritual significance. In religion, however, the household and other spirits are worshipped alongside Taoist deities adopted from the Chinese. This blending of a formal and highly evolved religion with the more usual worship of spirits is unique to the Mien (although, of course, some other tribes like the Karen and Lahu have more recently adopted Christianity).

The Taoist part of Mien worship involves considerable ritual and

(Top) An Akha village priest smoking a water pipe

(Middle) Seeds carved and drilled make a child's necklace

(Bottom) Young Akha girl in Chiang Rai province

sacred texts, and has also produced one of the most beautiful and interesting hilltribe artistic works - the sacred paintings. These are a set of 17 vertical pictures, a narrow scroll, and 11 smaller paintings. Some of the smaller pictures are worn on the head in some ceremonies. The subject of these sacred paintings, which take many weeks to make, is the hierarchy of Taoist gods. Some of them appear for sale in Thai antique shops: the genuine ones, which will all have been deconsecrated first, are sold by Mien families for whom religion is no longer so important, and sometimes because they have become worn and need to be replaced. There are both priests, for Taoist ceremonies, and shamans, who can be possessed by spirits.

LAHU

The Lahu are the third most numerous of the tribal groups in the hills of Thailand, and have migrated, originally from southwest China, via Burma's Shan States in the last hundred years. Called 'Mussur' by the Thais (a complimentary term that comes from Burmese and means 'hunter'), they are split into several sub-groups. Each of these - and there are four main groups in Thailand - is distinct in dress, dialect and customs. The names can be a source of confusion to a visitor, as they differ between English, Thai and what the Lahu call themselves. By far the largest sub-group is the Lahu Nyi, or Red Lahu; almost half of all Lahu in Thailand are members. The other three main sub-groups are the Lahu Na, Lahu Sheh Leh (both called Black Lahu in English) and Lahu Shi, or Yellow Lahu.

As with the Karen and Hmong, the English 'colour' names derive from the clothing. The dress of the Red Lahu, for example, has a predominance of red edging. These Lahu Nyi, and the Lahu Sheh Leh, generally continue to wear traditional dress, which the Lahu Na and longer-settled Lahu Shi now reserve for festivals and special occasions. The length of the woman's blouse or tunic varies between the groups: for Lahu Nyi and Lahu Shi it is short, for Lahu Sheh Leh three-quarter length, and for Lahu Na ankle-length. This is worn with a sarong-like skirt by all except the Lahu Sheh Leh, who wear culottes. Skillful embroidery is common to all Lahu.

In addition to local spirits - of the house, water, mountain and so on - the Lahu believe in a supreme God, called G'ui Sha. Indeed, the majority of Lahu Nyi villages have a temple consecrated to this deity. This belief in one being has certainly played an important part in the success that Christian missionaries have had in converting the Lahu. In Thailand, most Lahu Na and Lahu Shi villages are now Christian, and the Thai name for the Lahu Na is 'Lahu Khrit' (meaning Christian).

As with most other hilltribes, there is a strong feeling among the Lahu for conformity and unity within the village. However, as relatives are expected to support each other's claims and affairs (there are no clans among the Lahu), opposing factions are not uncommon in villages. The usual outcome of serious factional disputes is for one group of relatives to move out and live elsewhere. In the household, Lahu men have the reputation of being particularly considerate and helpful.

In the past, Lahu villages were settled in the upper levels of the hills, above 1200 metres. Nowadays, however, most have moved lower, with the exception of Lahu Sheh Leh settlements. Many of these higher villages still grow opium. As in most other hilltribe villages, most homes are built on stilts; there is a single door from the front porch into the main room, with a small bedroom inside. The Lahu Sheh Leh and Lahu Nyi have household altars.

AKHA

Despite having one of the smallest populations of all these peoples - about ten times less than the Karen - the Akha have in some ways come to symbolize the hilltribes in the popular imagination. One of the main reasons for this is the spectacular appearance of Akha girls and women, with their heavily ornamented peaked headdress and mini-skirt. Made from materials as diverse as beaten silver, gibbon fur, beads, seeds and feathered tassels, the Akha headdress appears like a helmet from some elaborate mythology, and is undoubtedly the crowning glory of hilltribe finery.

What is even more remarkable is that such an impressive headdress should be worn with such regularity. It would be easy to understand how an ornament like this could quickly be abandoned for all but ceremonial use - this, after all, is a trend seen throughout the hilltribes as they come into closer and closer contact with modern Thai life. Akha women, however, have no doubts about the appeal of their dress and its importance to their way of life. The headdress is by no means reserved for special occasions or worn for the benefit of tourists. Indeed, an Akha woman should only remove it for cleaning, repair, and for washing her hair.

The Akha headdress is, in fact, the most obvious outward example of the tribe's religious philosophy, known as the Akha Way. They themselves call it 'Akhazang' (the final consonant is nasal, with the 'g' unpronounced), and it permeates every aspect of their life, making the Akha the most conservative and traditional of all the hilltribes in Thailand. Akhazang is more than a religion; it is a social, moral and spiritual code that guides day-to-day living, from annual ceremonies to house-building, rice-planting and relationships with one another and with outsiders.

The current 'homeland' of the Akha is Yunnan, particularly in the region of Xishuangbanna, but they have migrated over the centuries into eastern Burma and Laos. Most of the Thai Akha have arrived from the Shan States, beginning at the turn of the century. The Thai name for them is quite derogatory: 'Eekaw', which broadly means 'low slave'. Not surprisingly, the Akha themselves resent this term. Of about 25,000 Akha in the country, more than nine-tenths live in Chiang Rai province.

The women's dress consists of a jacket, a simple blouse underneath that covers the breasts and midriff and is supported by a single string, a very short skirt, and leggings. This is completed by a sash with a front-piece hanging below the hem of the skirt, and the headdress. The cloth is woven by the Akha from cotton grown in their fields, and is dyed in indigo. Repeated dyeings produce the deep colour typical of Akha clothing - it can be almost black. It is also used for the appliqued and embroidered shoulder bags that have become a popular craft item sold to tourists in Chiang Mai's Night Bazaar and other places.

Although there are many more in Burma and in Yunnan, three distinctive Akha sub-groups are found in Thailand, identifiable mainly by the women's headdress. The most numerous are the U Lo-Akha, who wear the conical headdress and are the longest settled in the country. The second most common are the Loimi-Akha, named after a mountain in the Shan States ('Bear Mountain'); this style is characterised by a tapering flat plate of silver projecting upwards at the back, and by quantities of hollow silver balls. The third group is named after their principal settlement - Phami-Akha near Mae Sai in the far north of Chiang Rai Province - and wear a heavy, silver-covered helmet that is flat at the back with side-panels of overlapping silver coins. (Akha settlements, by the way, are always suffixed with '-Akha').

Faces from three generations of a Lisu village community

Over the basic structures of cloth reinforced with woven bamboo or wood, depending on the style, the chief ornament is silver. This is both in the form of silver coins and silver buttons, hemispheres or balls. These last are beaten out from coins by Akha silversmiths in holes drilled out of buffalo horn (the balls are two joined hemispheres). The amount of silver depends on the wealth of the family, and the economic difficulties that the Akha now share with other hilltribes is having an effect. Less silver is now being used, and aluminium is often substituted. Another reason for using aluminium is fear of being attacked and robbed outside the village: Akha women wear their headdresses even in the fields.

Other ornaments include hanging chains and pendants in silver, tassels made from chicken feathers dyed red, gibbon fur, beads of all kinds, and seeds from the forest. Much personal preference is involved in choosing items to hang from the headdress. It evolves through childhood and adolescence. At certain stages in growing up, the headdress and other items of clothing are changed.

Akha villages are built, whenever possible, on ridges. The houses are stilted, with enveloping thatched roofs that often reach the ground on the uphill side. Inside, there is a rigid division of use between the men's part of the house and the women's. Male visitors are not normally allowed in the women's section. There are no windows, so that the only natural illumination is from the doorway and the slats of the split-bamboo walls and floor. Each house contains an altar devoted to the family's ancestral spirits.

Other notable features of an Akha village are the spirit gates and the swing. On the paths above and below every village are ceremonial gates, alongside which are carved male and female figures. These gates act as a kind of barrier to the spirits outside the village and a way of purifying villagers returning from the forests. The gates and figures should on no account be touched by visitors, and the safest way of complying with Akha custom is to walk around them. Otherwise, if a visitor enters a village through a gate, it is obligatory to enter at least one house. The swing is erected and used once a year for a ceremony in which every member of the community swings on a seat attached to a vine.

The Akha believe in spirits both inside and outside the village, but also in a supreme deity, Apoe Miyeh. And, in common with the Karen, Lahu and some Hmong, they take care to propitiate the 'Lord of Land and Water' - the spiritual ruler of the locality.

As Akhazang, the Akha Way, plays such an important part in tribal life, its chief spokesmen are accorded special positions. The village leaders include the village priest, the blacksmith, the spirit priest, and village headman (who has secular responsibility and deals with the Thai authorities). In some villages there is also a shaman, capable of communicating directly with the spirit world in a trance.

The village economies of all the hilltribes owe more to the land and the climate than to any cultural differences, and everyday life follows much the same pattern from settlement to settlement. The rituals vary greatly, as does dress, but the communities must all support themselves with hill-rice, domesticated animals and whatever they can glean from the fast-disappearing forests. Fields have to be cleared on the hill-sides, rice pounded in the morning, pigs fed and roofs re-thatched. There are some differences - for instance, many Lisu villages grow opium and so are sited higher than others to be close to the 1,500 meters favoured by the poppy - but on the whole, the daily round is similar.

The problems, too, are similar, and all the hilltribes now face pressure on their cultures on a scale that they have never experienced before. The root of the problem is that all of these minorities are running out of the means of survival. There are no more hills and no more forests to which they can move. In an ideal hilltribe settlement, the village is surrounded by a 'green belt' of virgin forest, replete with old teak trees, plenty of game for the men to hunt, and a wealth of herbs and plants for medicine, food and dying cloth. Beyond this, patches of forest are cleared to make fields for the rice; they are cultivated for a year or two and then left fallow. This slash-and-burn cultivation has been condemned by many agronomists as ecologically destructive, but the practical truth is that the forests have always repaired themselves in the past - as long as there has been enough land.

Over the centuries, however, the tribes have migrated to avoid wars, conscription into armies and political unrest in general. Gradually, they have moved further and further along the ridges. Now, in Thailand, they have reached the end. From the airy platform of any number of tribal houses in northern Thailand, the view south is a pleasant panorama, looking out over the slopes to the wide plains in the distance. As far as the eye can see, the lowlands are planted with rice and dotted with hamlets and villages. The hilltribe dweller, however, sees something different from the tourist. All of the lowlands are planted with other people's rice. There is nowhere else to go. The ridges that dip gently into the broad valleys of Chiang Rai Province are the last fingers of the hill-country. There is not enough forest to allow old fields to grow back, and besides, illegal logging has denuded even more.

This is a time of change for all the hilltribes. Their traditional solution to difficulties by moving away is now hardly possible, and in some manner they must all accept a settled existence. Some communities will inevitably crumble and lose their identity, but it would be surprising if this were the fate of all. Hilltribe culture is as it is because of adversity, and there is a quality of resilience in the character of many of these peoples that has helped them adjust to difficult circumstances in the past. This, coupled with a feeling of tribal identity that is remarkably strong in some groups, may be sufficient to help them adapt to life in modern Thailand.

Tourism itself plays an increasingly important role, and one that is not necessarily harmful. In the past, Thai officials have often been irritated by the influx of peoples who are, for them, illegal immigrants, and puzzled to know how to deal with them. Now that tourism is booming, however, the hilltribes have become well-known internationally, and are actually a main tourist asset to Thailand. Of course, it is mainly the tourist industry that benefits financially, rather than the hilltribe communities who have a greater need for the money, but at least the new awareness of hilltribe culture has helped encourage the Thai authorities to take a more positive attitude. With luck, and economic support from their final adopted country, the hilltribes of Thailand may yet find a niche that allows them education, citizenship and a livelihood from farming without losing their cultural identity.

This Lisu girl carries her baby papoose-style. Being considered improper to allow babies to crawl, small children will be carried everywhere until they are large enough to walk.

Mist and low cloud partially hide the valley bottoms at sunrise. Near the border town of Mae Sai, the valley of the Mae Kok River (left) is farmed by Thais, and the dark limestone outcrops in the foreground mark the edge of hilltribe country. Further south in Chiang Rai Province (above), a succession of ridges is typical of the terrain settled by most groups.

(Following page) One of the more favorite locations for a village is the saddleback of a ridge at around 1000 meters (3300 feet). At this height the air is fresher than in the valleys and their are springs for the all important water supply. As much as possible, an area of forest is left untouched in the immediate vicinity of the village; the fields are out of sight in this aerial view. This mountain supports settlements from three different tribal groups: Lisu, Lahu, and Akha.

The materials used in building a hilltribe village are garnered from the surrounding forests: bamboo, wood, and grasses. These, and the exposed earth create the typically warm, brown earth tones of hill settlements. In the dark interiors of the houses, more forest products hang from walls and rafters; gourds, brooms, wicker baskets, and more. A good deal of village life is conducted in the open; while most people spend the days in the fields, some women (above) prepare roofing materials.

Although one of the poorest of the hilltribes in Thailand, the Akha stand out spectacularly in appearance, due mainly to the headdress of the women. Encrusted with as much silver as possible, it is worn almost permanently. The three styles that can be seen in Thailand identify the three sub-groups. The amount of silver worn by the Phami-Akha women (opposite) demonstrates her wealth. The back-plate worn by the women adjusting her leggings (above) is typical of the Loimi Akha. The most numerous are the U Lo-Akha: girls from this sub-group are giving a traditional massage to elders (top). Even young girls begin with a simple version of the headdress (right). There are approximately 25,000 Akhas in 155 villages in Thailand.

After the Karen, the Hmong (or 'Meo') are the most numerous of the hilltribes, (roughly numbering 60,000 in 246 settlements) and are now found in 13 of Thailand's seventy odd provinces. Characteristically, the women sweep their hair up into a bun; the black-and-white checkered cloth band worn at the hairline by the girl at left signifies that she is from the Blue Hmong. The men's pants are Chinese in style, but so full that they bear some resemblance at a distance to a long skirt (right).

While many of the Lahu, particularly those who have been converted by missionaries to Christianity, reserve traditional dress for special occasions, the Lahu Sheh Leh pictured here retain their customary clothing. Bath towels, however, have come to replace black cloth as the material of choice for turbans. This girl (below) is making an offering during an evening ceremony in the fenced ritual area of the village. The Lahu population numbers about 40,000 in 318 hamlets.

(Following page) Mien children in a village near Chiang Rai display finely embroidered panels on the front of their caps. Originating in southern China, where large numbers still live, the Mien, or Yao as they are called by the Thais or other hilltribes, moved into Thailand via Laos. Now just over 30,000 live in Thailand occupying 140 villages.

The Karen are by far the largest tribal group living in Thailand (roughly 250,000 people in over 2,000 settlements), although there are over 4 million living in Burma, from where they have immigrated. Nearly all are from either the Sgaw or Pwo branches, but a few Padaung families—instantly recognizable by the rack of neck rings worn by the women—have settled around Mae Hong Son. The bold red-and-white tunic worn by a 104 year old women in a village near Hot (right) is typical of Pwo Karen weaving. The turbanned Sgaw women (left) is chopping tobacco leaves.

Brightly-coloured clothes with a predominance of pale blue make Lisu women easy to spot even at a distance. The Lisu make up for being the smallest of the hilltribes in numbers (around 18,000 in 109 villages) by dressing the most flamboyantly. In their full ceremonial outfit, which includes a tasseled and beaded turban and great quantities of silver, the Lisu girls dressing for New Year festivities (left) are even more resplendent. Children wear miniature versions of adult tunics.

Most hilltribe houses are raised on stilts, as in the Lahu village (above left) and this Lisu dwelling (left). An obvious advantage of this method of construction is that it is easy to level the floor of the house even on a steep slope, but another immediately apparent advantage in the rainy season is that it raises the living area above the inevitable mud. The under-floor area becomes a general work space for pounding rice and other activities, and a shelter for domesticated animals. Kitchen refuse is received with gusto by the family pigs (left) which

patrol the ground for anything dropped through the split-bamboo floor. The Hmong, Mien and some Lisu, however, build directly on the ground. A packed earth floor like that in the Hmong household (top right) is typical of that kind of house, and tends to be warmer at higher, cooler altitudes. Verandas (bottom right), play an important role in daily life; as in this Akha house. The veranda becomes a focus for all kinds of activities, and a place to dry both food and washed clothing.

The most common thatching material is imperata grass, collected by the women from surrounding forests (above) and carried in bundles to the village (right) where it is laid on the roof in overlapping strips tied to battens (left). The thatching of new houses and re-thatching of existing ones is a dry season activity: once the rice has been harvested after the rains, there is time for general village chores before the next seasons rice needs to be planted. Although thatching is labor-intensive, it makes for a cooler, more comfortable dwelling than corrugated iron, which is becoming popular in some communities.

(Following page) House building is usually a communal activity. Stilted houses need a relatively complex structure of beams and posts—more than most families can easily build by themselves. And, in an economy that traditionally operates without money, the most workable system is that other members of the village help in the building in return for labor; often assistance in the building of _their_ new houses. With a large number of people working at the same time, most houses can be erected in one, or at the most two, days.

Totem figures are a special feature of Akha villages. On the paths leading downhill and uphill out of the village, a pair of figures is carved each year by the most skilled woodworker in the village. The figures vary greatly in the quality of their carving, but there is always a male and a female. Some are embellished, for instance with a pipe or other everyday accoutrements; the female figure on the right of the pair above has been given the back-plate typical of a Loimi Akha headdress. Positioned by the village's two gates, these figures are accompanied by star-like bamboo constructions, which are taboos, and representations of birds. Previous years' figures are never removed—they are simply allowed to rot.

Rice is the mainstay of all the village economies and the sight of women and girls pounding and winnowing is an essential part of the experience of life in a hilltribe community. Indeed, the first human sound of the day, well before sunrise, is the thudding of treadle operated rice pounders that are usually located under the houses (top). Not surprisingly, rice has a spiritual significance as well, and newly harvested rice (left) is, in some communities, placed in a sacred shelter (above).

Opium, grown both for direct use and for the production of heroin, is the traditional cash crop of the Golden Triangle. It needs the elevation of the hills in which the tribes live, and although it is labor-intensive (right) it is very valuable. During the growing season, at the end of the monsoon rains, the pod is incised so that the opium appears as oozing, sticky beads which are then scraped off (top). A problem for many hilltribe people is addiction (above) while the Thai authorities are trying to combat cultivation with crop-substitution programs. Indeed, opium production in Thailand has fallen off to about 15 tons per annum compared to 500-1000 tons still produced in Burma and Laos.

The structure of the hill villages keeps man and animals in a close relationship. The most common domesticated animals are chickens and pigs for food, dogs for hunting and gaurding the house (the Akha also eat them) and pack horses for transport. The underfloor area of stilted houses is a convenient shelter for most of these animals, so that they are very much part of the household. The Karen, normally, are the only tribe to catch and train elephants (left). The mahout then hires himself and his charge out to loggers, while the elephant is also useful for work around the village.

The bulk of the women's daily work is in some way connected with food and water. Squashes, (right) and other vegetables are grown in lots close to the houses, while other plants (above) are collected from the forests. Water often has to be drawn from a distance, although the construction of bamboo aqueducts (left) is one ingenious solution. Most cooking is done over an open hearth inside the house, as in this Lisu interior.

Hunting is the province of men, and traditionally game from the forest would be an important part of the diet. The weapon of choice is a home-made long barreled muzzle-loader. Lead shot bought from a Thai store is poured into the muzzle (left), and tamped down with a wad of cotton (right). In this case, the ignition mechanism (above) uses the caps made for a child's toy pistol. Game is now scarce, and birds and squirrels are the most common catch.

In the lower elevations of the hills, the rivers are large enough to fish. One method, shown above, is a hand-net, cast with weighted edges. Hooks and woven fish traps are also used. An alternative to guns is the crossbow—quieter in use but not so effective over distance. The skulls of animals killed are often attached to a post in the hunter's house; that at left is a porcupine.

(Following page) In the early morning mist, a hunter passes the sacred upper gate of an Akha village on his way to the forest. The depletion of game in recent decades means that he will probably return to the village with only a few small animals.

The helmet-like headdresses of the Akha women receive an enormous amount of attention—and expense. One of the rare occasions on which it is removed is for cleaning and repair (below). Seen from behind, the tapering back-plate of a Loimi Akha headdress takes on an abstract appearance (top).

The basic structure of the headdress is cloth, sewn with pieces of silver, and reinforced in this U Lo-Akha style with a framework of woven bamboo. This is by no means the end of the decoration, however. Chicken feathers are dyed red, tufts are made from the fur of gibbons, and items ranging from seeds to beads are added. Tiny gourds (top) show that the wearer is unmarried. The chicken feathers are tied to lengths of string and teased into tassels (below).

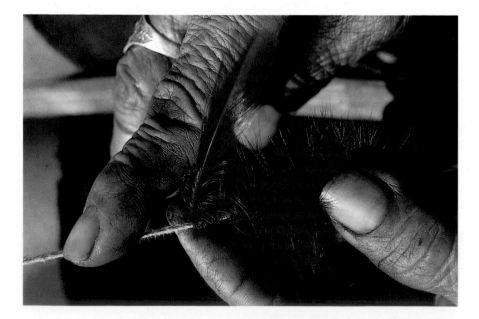

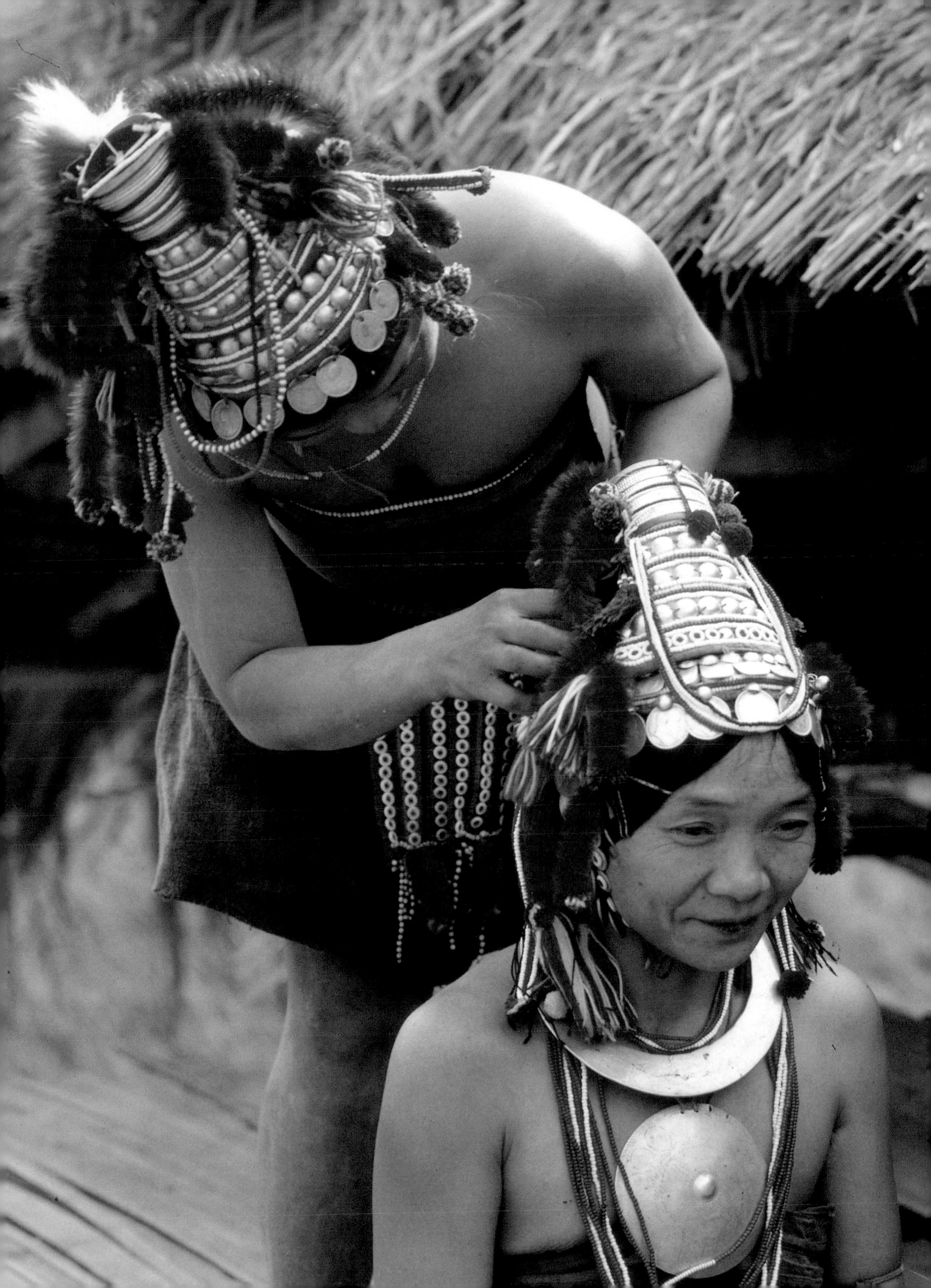

Silver is the repository of hilltribe wealth, and is worn as jewellery. Old silver coins, from India, Burma, French Indochina, China and Thailand, have traditionally been an important source of the metal for village silversmiths. This is unfortunately a skill which is fast disappearing; the silversmith (left) is beating a coin into a rounded button, using a buffalo horn that has been drilled with deep, smooth holes. Silver buttons of all kinds are an important decoration for much hilltribe clothing (right).

Considerable effort goes into the making and adornment of clothing, from the ubiquitous silver to all kinds of embroidery and appliqué. This work occupies most of the spare time of tribal women and is a highly developed craft that in recent years has begun to generate a supplementary income from sales of jackets, shoulder bags and panels to tourists. One of the more esoteric kinds of embellishment is from insects—the iridescent wing-cases of green beetles (left), make pendants attached to a man's jacket.

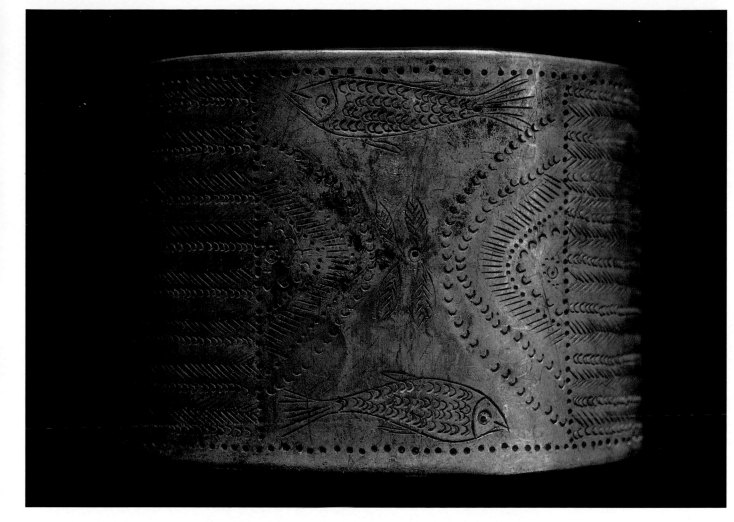

Silver is also worked into items larger than buttons, although most of the good, genuine pieces are actually quite old. Bracelets, like the flat design above, were most commonly bought from Chinese silversmiths and pre-date the migrations into Thailand. Silver pipes are also usually Chinese in origin (and in style), although some were made in the Shan states of Burma.

The elaborate silver pendants worn
by Lisu women (left) feature tiers of
chains and silver tassels. Some, like
that shown here, feature Chinese
cloisonné work, with fish being a
common motif. A Lahu man wears
a hooked earring (right), while
a cowrie shell and a modern British
copper coin have been improvised into
a child's necklace (bottom right).

Basketry is an important village craft, employing mainly bamboo and rattan. Fast-growing bamboo is, in fact, the most commonplace construction material found in the hills and is used in everything from houses, bridges, and fences to delicately woven items. Increasingly, hilltribe basket makers are finding a ready market for their products in the local towns and in Chiang Mai.

Of all the rites of passage, funerals tend to be the most elaborate and significant—the dead person is returning to the land of the ancestors. In the funeral of an Akha elder, the coffin is painstakingly hewn from a single log. The origins of its curved, boat-like shape and its projections are lost even to the Akha themselves. After the spirit priest, called the pi ma, has performed the death rites for three days (below), the coffin is carried uphill from the village by the young men to its secret burial site. A buffalo is slaughtered, and then covered with unhusked rice (left).

The evening is normally the only time for relaxation. After a day in the fields, the oil lamps are lit and fires stoked. A young Lisu man sings wistfully of courtship, accompanying himself on a simple stringed instrument. A group of children play on the open ground in the middle of a village (below), while an old woman (right) gazes contentedly into the hearth at the end of dinner. A few people stay up gossiping until well after sundown, but for most members of the village work must start again early the next morning and sleep comes quickly and easily.